Keep this pocket-sized Fri~~th book with you when~~
you are travelling around the coasts of South Devon.

Whether you are in your car or on foot, you will
enjoy an evocative journey back in time. Compare
the South Devon of old with what you can see
today—see how the streets have changed, how shops
and buildings have been altered or replaced, how
seaside resorts and fishing harbours have developed
and expanded; look at fine details such as
lamp-posts, shop fascias and trade signs. See the
many alterations to South Devon that have taken
place during our lives, and which we may have
taken for granted.

At the turn of a page you will gain fascinating
insights into South Devon's unique history.

FRANCIS FRITH'S
pocket ALBUM

SOUTH DEVON COAST

A POCKET ALBUM

Adapted from an original book by
JOHN BAINBRIDGE

FRITH
BOOK Co

First published in the United Kingdom in 2003 by
Frith Book Company Ltd

ISBN 1-85937-715-7

Text and Design copyright © Frith Book Company Ltd
Photographs copyright © The Francis Frith Collection

The Frith photographs and the Frith logo are reproduced under licence from Heritage
Photographic Resources Ltd, the owners of the Frith archive and trademarks

British Library Cataloguing in Publication Data

South Devon Coast—A Pocket Album
Adapted from an original book by John Bainbridge

Frith Book Company Ltd
Frith's Barn, Teffont,
Salisbury, Wiltshire SP3 5QP
Tel: +44 (0) 1722 716 376
Email: info@francisfrith.co.uk
www.francisfrith.co.uk

Printed and bound in Great Britain by MPG, Bodmin

Front Cover: Teignmouth The Parade 1903 / 49559 *The colour-tinting is for illustrative
purposes only, and is not intended to be historically accurate.*

Frontispiece: Teignmouth, The Beach 1903 / 49560

CONTENTS

FRANCIS FRITH
VICTORIAN PIONEER

*Francis Frith, founder of the world-famous photographic
archive, was a complex and multi-talented man. A devout
Quaker and a highly successful Victorian businessman, he was philosophic
by nature and pioneering in outlook. By 1855 he had already established a
wholesale grocery business in Liverpool, and sold it for the astonishing sum
of £200,000, which is the equivalent today of over £15,000,000. Now in
his thirties, and captivated by the new science of photography, Frith set out
on a series of pioneering journeys up the Nile and to the Near East.*

INTRIGUE AND EXPLORATION

He was the first photographer to venture beyond the sixth cataract of the
Nile. Africa was still the mysterious 'Dark Continent', and Stanley and
Livingstone's historic meeting was a decade into the future. The conditions
for picture taking confound belief. He laboured for hours in his wicker dark-
room in the sweltering heat of the desert, while the volatile chemicals fizzed
dangerously in their trays. Back in London he exhibited his photographs and
was 'rapturously cheered' by members of the Royal Society. His reputation as
a photographer was made overnight.

VENTURE OF A LIFE-TIME

By the 1870s the railways had threaded their way across the country, and
Bank Holidays and half-day Saturdays had been made obligatory by Act of
Parliament. All of a sudden the working man and his family were able to
enjoy days out, take holidays, and see a little more of the world.

With typical business acumen, Francis Frith foresaw that these new
tourists would enjoy having souvenirs to commemorate their days out. For

the next thirty years he travelled the country by train and by pony and trap, producing fine photographs of seaside resorts and beauty spots that were keenly bought by millions of Victorians. These prints were painstakingly pasted into family albums and pored over during the dark nights of winter, rekindling precious memories of summer excursions. Frith's studio was soon supplying retail shops all over the country, and by 1890 F Frith & Co had become the greatest specialist photographic publishing company in the world, with over 2,000 sales outlets, and pioneered the picture postcard.

FRANCIS FRITH'S LEGACY

Francis Frith had died in 1898 at his villa in Cannes, his great project still growing. The archive he created continued in business for another seventy years. By 1970 it contained over a third of a million pictures showing 7,000 British towns and villages.

Frith's legacy to us today is of immense significance and value, for the magnificent archive of evocative photographs he created provides a unique record of change in the cities, towns and villages throughout Britain over a century and more. Frith and his fellow studio photographers revisited locations many times down the years to update their views, compiling for us an enthralling and colourful pageant of British life and character.

We are fortunate that Frith was dedicated to recording the minutiae of everyday life. For it is this sheer wealth of visual data, the painstaking chronicle of changes in dress, transport, street layouts, buildings, housing, engineering and landscape that captivates us so much today, offering us a powerful link with the past and with the lives of our ancestors.

Computers have now made it possible for Frith's many thousands of images to be accessed almost instantly. The archive offers every one of us an opportunity to examine the places where we and our families have lived and worked down the years. Its images, depicting our shared past, are now bringing pleasure and enlightenment to millions around the world a century and more after his death.

SOUTH DEVON COAST
FROM AXMOUTH TO PLYMOUTH

To travel along Devon's south coast is to participate in a journey of many delights, whether you undertake the long trek on foot along the South Devon Coastal Footpath, from Plymouth to the Dorset border at Lyme Regis, or go by car or public transport from village to village and town to town.

In spite of its popularity with generations of holidaymakers, much of the coast remains unexplored except by the few. There are great stretches of high cliff, lonely beaches, wild and unspoiled interior countryside and quaint fishing villages to seek out.

Even the city of Plymouth does not yet overwhelm the pastoral countryside of the South Hams, and it has its own delightful walks and dramatic areas of coastline. The increasingly large conurbation of Torbay is still broken up by some attractive pieces of countryside, though these now seem to be under siege from modern development.

In Teignbridge and East Devon we have two of the oldest seaside resorts in the county—Teignmouth and Exmouth. Their layout tells us much about the development of the holiday industry in Britain. They also have the considerable merit of being surrounded by some of the finest scenery along the coast.

The Frith photographers caught these urban and rural landscapes before the character of the towns was compromised by massive building programmes and the dominance of the motor car. But if these pictures are an illustration of things lost, they are also useful pointers to the better parts of the South Devon coast which remain—seek these out and enjoy them.

SIDMOUTH 1907 / 58062

DEVONPORT

TORPOINT FERRY BRIDGE 1890 / 22462

PLYMOUTH AND THE SOUTH HAMS

THE PLYMOUTH we see today is not the city that residents and visitors would have known before the Second World War. Even by the standards of the worst wartime blitzes Plymouth suffered badly, being devastated beyond recognition. The heart of the old Victorian town was torn out, mostly during one terrible night. All we have to remember the old Plymouth by is archive film, photographs such as the ones that follow, and the memories of survivors.

Not all of the old city was lost. A stroll through the Barbican to Sutton Harbour, which the bombs mostly spared, gives a feel of old Plymouth town as Drake might have known it. But ten thousand other old buildings were destroyed, and seventy thousand more were damaged by high explosive and firestorm. It says a lot for the indomitable spirit of the people of Plymouth that after the bombing of St Andrews church, a painted wooden notice had appeared over its doorway bearing the single word RESURGAM—I shall rise again!

Plymouth did rise again, though few who remembered the old town were happy with the new. Yet some old landmarks are still there. Locals meet at Derry's Cross as they always did. Sailors continue to throng Union Street on Saturday nights. Tourists still make a first stop at Plymouth Hoe to see the spot where Sir Francis Drake may or may not have played a famous game of bowls.

Within a bus journey of the city centre is some of the loveliest pastoral scenery in England. The South Hams is a wondrous collection of ancient towns, picturesque villages and spectacular coastal scenery, remaining fiercely independent of the great city not far away. The absence of major roads to the coast, the inspiring walks and probably the mildest climate in mainland Britain, bring visitors back again and again. Caught between Plymouth and the Dart estuary in one direction and Dartmoor and the coast in the other, the South Hams have an identity and character all their own.

Its towns are modest in size and as old as history. Kingsbridge is mostly Saxon in origin, though Iron Age man lived not far away. The twisting Kingsbridge estuary is reminiscent of the mysterious and muddy creeks of southern Cornwall, rather than anywhere else in Devon. Salcombe, the port at its mouth, seems to live for sailing, with a happy flotilla of yachts, dinghies and motor boats exploring the tidal waters on calm days.

Dartmouth, some miles east, climbs the steep hillside above its own estuary. This is a naval town where officers from all over the world are trained. It has a long connection with the sea. Crusaders, privateers, naval armadas and D-Day invasion forces all set sail from here. The Dart estuary, surely Devon's most beautiful one, is navigable as far as Totnes, before it becomes a rushing watercourse winding up to Dartmoor. Agatha Christie lived on its banks at Greenway House, high above the ferry crossing at Dittisham, for many years.

Many consider that the stretch of coastline between Thurlestone and the Dart to be the finest in England. But it can be a cruel coast as well. Its high rocky cliffs have been the downfall of many ships, their wrecks littering the seabed just offshore. The coastline west of the Dart has sad recent memories. Several villages inland from Slapton Sands were evacuated during the Second World War, and the surrounding countryside was given over to the United States Army. Hundreds of young American soldiers and sailors died here and in Lyme Bay rehearsing for the D-Day landings. A stone obelisk and a recovered Sherman Tank near the great freshwater lake of Slapton Ley records their deeds and honours their sacrifice.

Now all is peaceful; the cry of the birds, the crash of the waves and the sough of the warm summer breeze have drowned out the horrendous noise of shot and shell. The South Hams too have 'risen again', managing to capture a peace and tranquillity perhaps more in keeping with Edwardian times than with the rush of a new Millennium.

As an important naval port, Plymouth has always had a large contingent of military personnel stationed around its various districts. Many impressive buildings, such as the barracks shown here, have been built to accommodate them.

DEVONPORT

ROYAL MARINE BARRACKS, STONEHOUSE 1890 / 22448

Below the fortifications of Mount Wise we can see a variety of shipping, from paddle steamers to ancient naval vessels, which were probably used as training depots. These seem to have more in common with Nelson's navy than with the iron-clad battleships that were starting to dock at Devonport at this time.

DEVONPORT

MOUNT WISE 1890 / 22468

It is probable that Devonport abandoned its earlier name of Plymouth Dock as a gesture of independence. A huge community, both military and trading, grew around the naval yards with thousands of homes to cater for dockworkers and public houses in which to entertain shorebound sailors.

DEVONPORT

HALFPENNY BRIDGE 1904 / 52427

PLYMOUTH

UNION STREET 1889 / 22359

Union Street, famous to sailors throughout the world, is the high road from Devonport to Plymouth. Even in Victorian times it had a wild reputation, but it reached the zenith of its colourful activities in the 20th century.

Serving both a rural area round about, and hundreds of overseas ports by way of trade, Plymouth reached its mercantile heyday in Victorian times. For many years the Great Western Railway ended its journey at the city. Only with the construction of the Royal Albert Bridge across the Tamar to Saltash did the railway open up the Duchy of Cornwall.

PLYMOUTH

GEORGE STREET 1889 / 22397

The Tavistock road leads away from Plymouth to the fringes of Dartmoor, and has always been a busy highway. The supply of a great city in Victorian times called for the support of hundreds of local farmers, who would bring in endless amounts of food and other goods.

PLYMOUTH

TAVISTOCK ROAD 1890 / 22423

PLYMOUTH

THE BARBICAN 1890 / 22474

The Barbican lines Sutton Harbour, long a fishing quay and the original port of Plymouth. From here Elizabethan sailors, merchants and privateers would have set sail in search of profit and adventure on the high seas.

Plymouth never quite achieved the status of being a major seaside resort, though tourists have always bathed from its beaches and promenaded across the famous Hoe. The City's holiday value is as a touring centre. There are many delightful coves and coastal walks in the vicinity.

PLYMOUTH

THE PIER 1898 / 41930

Below Plymouth Hoe, where legend tells us that Sir Francis Drake played that famous game of bowls, is a promenade for strolling or lounging on deckchairs. It is also an excellent viewpoint from which to watch ships entering and leaving Plymouth Sound.

PLYMOUTH

THE LIDO AND WALKS 1934 / 86216

A charming study of two young onion sellers taken by the Frith photographer during the long and prosperous 'Edwardian Afternoon'. Merchant ships brought goods from all over the world into Plymouth's harbours.

PLYMOUTH

ONION SELLERS 1907 / 59208

Yealmpton, always pronounced Yampton, stands on the River Yealm near to the end of its short journey from Dartmoor to the sea. The church is very much a Victorian restoration, but has some excellent old tombs, particularly the 17th-century one for Mary Copleston, whose effigy is surrounded by three of her seven children.

YEALMPTON

FROM THE BRIDGE 1904 / 52428

Newton Ferrers and Noss Mayo, 'Newton and Noss' to all locals, line the opposite banks of the Yealm estuary. Both are delightful, with old Devon cob cottages and attractive gardens in an area of fine scenery. It is hard to imagine the crowded streets of Plymouth only a few miles away.

NEWTON FERRERS

BRIDGE END 1931 / 83975

Noss Mayo's church, seen in the middle distance, was built on the orders of Lord Revelstoke in 1882 in a beautiful setting above both the village and river. The original parish church is now a picturesque ruin some distance away on the clifftops of Stoke Point.

NOSS MAYO

RIVER YEALM 1901 / 46327

BIGBURY-ON-SEA

THE VILLAGE 1925 / 78342

Bigbury-on-Sea lies on the shores of Bigbury Bay within site of Burgh Island, which may give the village its name. Many famous people such as Agatha Christie, who set novels in the locality, Noel Coward and Edward VIII stayed on Burgh Island and walked this wild coastline.

BIGBURY-ON-SEA

FROM CLIMATON HILL 1924 / 76565

The tiny settlement of Bantham, with its passenger ferry and boat-houses, clings to the eastern bank of the Avon where the river makes one last sweeping curve before meeting the sea.

BANTHAM

1926 / 78324

Thurlestone takes its name from a holed, or thirled, rock just out at sea in Bigbury Bay, which was mentioned in a Saxon charter way back in 845. Despite some garish modern buildings and the large golf course nearby, Thurlestone remains the attractive village we see here in 1918.

THURLESTONE

THE VILLAGE 1918 / 68605

Hope Cove was a simple fishing village cut off from the world until it was 'discovered' in the 20th century. It says a lot for its resilience that it has remained unspoiled, remaining a wonderful place to visit and to get away from the pressures of modern life.

HOPE COVE

COTTAGES 1890 / 25260

Hope Cove remains one of the few safe anchorages between the Yealm estuary and Salcombe, several miles to the east. Tiny fishing smacks still set out from the cove each day, much as they probably did in 1588 when the Spanish Armada was first sighted off the Devon coast.

HOPE COVE

1904 / 52467

Much of this bare hillside between Outer and Inner Hope has now been built upon, but the tiny church remains and the coast nearby is wild and spectacular. Around the next headland is Ramillies Cove where HMS Ramillies was wrecked two centuries ago, with the loss of over 700 lives.

HOPE COVE

1925 / 78392

Malborough lies away from the coast, high above the Salcombe estuary, but it is an ideal place to stay when exploring the beautiful stretch of coastline between Bolt Head and Bolt Tail—the favourite scenery of many Devonians.

MALBOROUGH

LOWER TOWN 1927 / 79903

Salcombe is a small port at the mouth of the
Kingsbridge estuary. It is so sheltered and mild that
even oranges have been known to grow there. The town
has become a haven for leisure yachtsmen, with many
of its shops devoted to water sports and its old inns
occupied by the sailing fraternity.

SALCOMBE

THE QUAYSIDE 1896 / 38483

Salcombe was the home of the Victorian historian James Anthony
Froude, author of a history of England and of biographical publications
about Thomas and Jane Carlyle. His approach to English history was
extremely partisan and often factually doubtful, though always readable.
Froude is buried in the church cemetery.

SALCOMBE

FORE STREET 1907 / 58775

SALCOMBE

GULLET 1922 / 73255

A timeless scene in one of the many creeks of the long estuary that runs between Salcombe and Kingsbridge. The wooded banks of this stretch of water are best explored by boat at high tide, though even at low tide the extensive mud flats are home to a huge variety of birdlife.

Local tradition alleges that Alfred, Lord Tennyson wrote his famous poem 'Crossing the Bar' with the perilous entrance to the Salcombe estuary in mind. He certainly visited the town, though it has to be said that several other ports claim the honour of possessing the sand bar in question.

SALCOMBE

GENERAL VIEW 1920 / 69808

A few ruined walls in the estuary mark the site of Fort Charles, which was garrisoned by the royalist army for four months in 1646 during the English Civil War. So bravely did they defend this hopeless position in the face of a mightier parliamentarian army that the Roundhead commander allowed them to leave with colours flying.

SALCOMBE

FROM PORTLEMOUTH 1928 / 81014

A bridge crossed the head of the Kingsbridge estuary as early as 962, though the surviving bridges in the area are medieval in origin. Notice the ghostly boat below the right-hand side of the bridge, evidence of the slow exposure of the photograph.

KINGSBRIDGE

THE BRIDGE 1890 / 24525

KINGSBRIDGE

TACKETT WOOD COTTAGES 1896 / 38428

Tackett or Ticket Wood is said to get its name from the
nonconformists who worshipped here illegally centuries
ago. Tradition suggests that tickets would be issued for
these meetings by worshippers so as to avoid infiltration
by spies, who might betray them to the authorities.

A steep hill leads away from the estuary to the top of Kingsbridge town. The settlement here was probably established in Saxon times, though it did not become an important trading centre until the Abbot of Buckfast established a market here in 1219. Within a few years Kingsbridge and the adjoining manor of Dodbrooke achieved borough status.

KINGSBRIDGE

FORE STREET 1896 / 38429

Kingsbridge boasts several famous sons: they include William Cookworthy, who discovered that English china clay could be used to make porcelain, and John Hicks, the protestant preacher who marched to Sedgemoor with Monmouth's rebels in 1685.

KINGSBRIDGE

FORE STREET 1918 / 68604

KINGSBRIDGE

THE RIVER 1920 / 69826

Legend relates that a Saxon king, on a progress through his realm, wondered how he could cross a creek without getting his feet wet. An obliging servant stepped into the water offering to piggy-back the king across —hence Kingsbridge. The parish church, seen here in the distance, is dedicated to St Edmund the Martyr.

48

During the Second World War villagers were evacuated from many villages around the South Hams so that the district could become a D-Day training ground for American soldiers, who would practise troop landings on Slapton Sands. More Americans died training here than were killed on Utah Beach on D-Day.

TORCROSS

THE SANDS 1896 / 38438

Slapton was one of the villages evacuated during the war. Villagers were given only a few days to pack up their belongings and move away. Many buildings were damaged during the exercises but now, happily, show few scars. An obelisk, a gift from the United States Army, can be seen on the nearby sands, its plaque offering thanks to the villagers for their sacrifice.

SLAPTON

THE POST OFFICE 1925 / 78245

DARTMOUTH

NEW QUAY 1890 / 25289

Dartmouth has always been a port for adventurers and plunderers. Crusaders gathered here to sail with Richard the Lionheart. Privateers left from the town to plunder French and Spanish ports. Soldiers sailed in June 1944 for the invasion of Normandy.

Queen Victoria much admired the town of Dartmouth and its beautiful estuary, recording in her journal that '... the place is lovely, with its wooded rocks and church and castle at the entrance. It puts me so much in mind of the beautiful Rhine ...'

DARTMOUTH

DARTMOUTH REGATTA 1889 / 21648

DARTMOUTH

THE ROYAL NAVAL COLLEGE 1918 / 68612A

Generations of British naval officers have trained in this impressive building, or on the old ships moored here in the days before the land base was established. It was here that Princess Elizabeth, later Queen Elizabeth II, first met her husband Prince Phillip.

DARTMOUTH

DITTISHAM, ON THE DART 1889 / 21617

TORBAY AND TEIGNBRIDGE

IN ADMIRAL Nelson's day it was said that the entire British naval fleet could take shelter in Torbay during stormy weather. On calmer days the bay was used as a supply depot for ships participating in the blockade of France during the Napoleonic Wars. Among the first visitors to the area were the wives and families of serving officers, who took up residence in Torquay so as to be near their loved ones.

Napoleon Bonaparte must have appreciated Torbay's strategic importance as he paced the decks of HMS Bellerophon: it lay anchored off Torquay before the deposed Emperor was shipped to his last exile on St Helena. Napoleon, basking in the interest of the crowds who came out by boat to catch a glimpse of him, famously compared the bay to the best parts of Italy and Elba.

The bay's three major resorts are all very different from each other in character. Brixham remains a charming old fishing town, beloved of artists, photographers and the tourists who throng the quay in the summer to watch the trawlers come and go. It is the most unspoiled of the towns, and glories in its rugged and romantic setting. Paignton, in contrast, is a happy family resort, with two miles of safe bathing on golden sandy beaches. The Singer family's residence in Paignton, and the construction of the imposing Oldway Mansion, raised the profile of the resort across the country, and the tourists flooded in.

If you look down from one of its many hilltops, Torquay gives the impression of having grown out of the twisted limestone on which it rests, its elegant buildings clinging to the peaks, slopes and hollows of a wild and broken landscape. If it has not always succeeded in its aim to be an upmarket watering place, it has at least weathered the vagaries of the 20th century with some considerable flair and dignity. A walk around its steep and winding streets reveals much about both the social history of holiday resorts and the *longer story of those who worked the land before the tourists arrived. Its chosen title, 'Queen of the English Riviera', is deserved, for much of the old town exudes a regal charm.*

A walk or sail eastwards brings the traveller to the estuaries of the Teign and the Exe. The land between is Teignbridge, though the name is a political rather a geographical delineation. At its heart is the market town of Newton Abbot—the focus for shoppers throughout the district. This community was old even before 1688 when William of Orange marched through on his journey to the British throne; it was an ancient monastic holding, as its name implies.

BRIXHAM

INNER HARBOUR 1889 / 21552

Following the Teign estuary downstream brings us to Teignmouth, Devon's second oldest holiday resort and still a popular place for day-trippers. This old settlement has been battered by history, for almost every enemy of England throughout the last two millennia seems to have raided and burnt it down. Unkind planners in the last century have not always done their best by Teignmouth, but somehow it has survived; the fact that its best parts remain so little changed since these photographs were taken says a great deal for its durability.

Dawlish is a delight, a charming regency town, with Brunel's railway running along its sea-front in what must surely be one of the most picturesque journeys in England. Black swans cadge food as they swim up and down the Dawlish Water, that charming brook dividing the town, and summer bathers enjoy the mile of sand that runs to Dawlish Warren.

Torbay and Teignbridge are the most urbanised and crowded sections of the South Devon coast, and their delights are not always as obvious as those on the wilder coastlines of East Devon or the South Hams. But a little exploration reveals much about the character and development of this part of the county, and a great deal about the evolution of the English seaside resort.

BRIXHAM

FISHING BOATS 1889 / 21558

This idyllic picture of the Brixham fishing fleet in the late 19th century gives some idea of just how much the fishing industry dominated the town for hundreds of years. At the height of the Victorian age some 200 trawlers would regularly put to sea from the harbour at Brixham.

William of Orange, whose statue looks away from the sea and towards England, landed at Brixham on 5 November 1688 to depose the Catholic King James II and to herald 'a glorious revolution'. William and his Dutch troops received a hearty welcome from local families.

BRIXHAM

THE PRINCE OF ORANGE MONUMENT 1891 / 28241

The fishermen of Brixham refined the technique of trawling for their catch close to the bottom of the sea; this technique mostly replaced the earlier drifting. The sailing trawlers needed to work with the tide and a stiff wind—up to force six or seven —behind them if the nets were to be trawled successfully.

BRIXHAM

GENERAL VIEW 1896 / 38882

BRIXHAM
INNER HARBOUR 1906 / 54039

Until the 20th-century, shipbuilding was Brixham's most important industry after fishing. Small merchant vessels and privateers were constructed during earlier times for trade and piracy, though in later years many of the shipbuilders concentrated on building and repairing fishing boats.

BRIXHAM

THE HARBOUR 1925 / 78492

BRIXHAM

THE HARBOUR 1925 / 78490

*Paignton pier, one of the oldest in Britain, strides 800 feet out to sea;
we see it here in all its Victorian finery. Of all the Torbay resorts, only
Paignton has a pier, owing to a combination of its great popularity as a
family resort and the gently sloping sands that made possible the pier's
construction.*

PAIGNTON

THE PIER 1889 / 21529

Paignton's harbour is an extension of a simple early shelter for shipping. Though not as protected from rough and stormy seas as the harbour at Brixham, it maintained a fishing fleet for several centuries. It is used today mostly for leisure boating.

PAIGNTON

THE HARBOUR 1890 / 25907

PAIGNTON

Paignton became fashionable with the arrival of the Singer family, who built Oldway Mansion in 1874. The sewing machine millionaires completed their home in 1907, inspired by the architectural wonders of Versailles. The cream of Victorian society visited the Singers at their imposing seaside home.

PAIGNTON

THE PROMENADE AND SANDS 1907 / 58415A

PAIGNTON

CHURCH STREET 1912 / 64719

St John's Church at Paignton originally dated from the 12th century, but was rebuilt three hundred years later. It is said to stand on the site of a Bronze Age burial mound. The Kirkham chapel within contains the tombs of Sir William Kirkham and his wife, who died in the 17th century.

PAIGNTON

PRESTON SANDS 1918 / 68533

This photograph shows a Torbay at war. Seaplanes from the newly-formed Royal Air Force are pulled up on the beach—perhaps being used either for recruitment or anti-submarine duties. There is a marked absence of young men—they are all away at the Front.

PAIGNTON

THE HARBOUR 1922 / 73067

The picture-postcard village of Cockington forms a green oasis between the urban sprawls of Paignton and Torquay. The thatched building on the left is the famous Cockington Forge.

TORQUAY

COCKINGTON 1901 / 47821

Before the coming of tourism, Torquay was an obscure fishing hamlet, its villagers scratching a living from the sea, smuggling and lime burning. All of these activities continued well into the Victorian age.

TORQUAY

BEACON TERRACE 1888 / 21428

St John's Church, sited dramatically above Torquay harbour, was built
in limestone excavated from its own site by the architect G E Street
in 1861. Its west window was designed by the pre-Raphaelite artist
Edward Burne-Jones. The church is said to be haunted by the ghosts
of two former organists, whose music can still be heard echoing over
the town.

TORQUAY

THE HARBOUR 1890 / 25921

The elegant Abbey Crescent was built in 1858 in anticipation of the opening of the nearby railway station the following year. Its designers considered that this new access to Torquay would help popularise this hitherto quiet end of town.

TORQUAY

ABBEY CRESCENT 1896 / 38598

TORQUAY

FROM VANE HILL 1901 / 47806

*An early visitor said of Torquay: 'It is not England, but
a bit of sunny Italy taken bodily from its rugged coast
and placed here amid the green places and the pleasant
pastoral lanes of beautiful Devon'.*

Apart from a considerable increase in traffic, Torquay's Strand has changed very little since this photograph was taken in Edwardian times. The harbour was at that time still the preserve of local fishermen, but today the area is monopolised by pleasure craft and luxury yachts.

TORQUAY

THE STRAND 1906 / 54015

TORQUAY

PRINCESS PARADE 1920 / 69579

In the 1920s Torquay became not only a venue for family holidays but a much-loved destination for day trips, with tourists arriving by train and charabanc. Air raids in the Second World War led to the decline in Torquay harbour's use as a commercial port, though ferries have continued to ply their trade to the Channel Islands from here. The harbour marina is now full of luxury yachts.

TORQUAY

THE STRAND 1920 / 69586

On a crowded summer's day, sunbathers enjoy the warmth on Abbey sands. Modesty dictated that bathers should get changed in one of the long line of changing tents.

TORQUAY

ABBEY SANDS 1924 / 76401

One of a number of attractive coves on the length of beautiful coastline between Torquay and Babbacombe, Anstey's Cove has been a favourite retreat for holidaymakers since Victorian times, when the proprietor would provide cream teas and swimming lessons for patrons.

TORQUAY

ANSTEY'S COVE 1896 / 38609

Early visitors faced a long climb back up to Babbacombe after a day on the beaches, but in the 1920s a cliff railway— still in use today—was built, making the journey up the cliff much easier.

TORQUAY

ODDICOMBE BEACH 1889 / 21491

Before the development of Babbacombe as a small holiday resort, its isolated coves were used by smugglers such as Bob Elliott of Brixham and Jack Rattenbury of Beer. The present coastal footpath came into being as a patrol route for the coast-guards, whose duty it was to intercept illicit cargoes.

BABBACOMBE

THE DOWNS 1918 / 68547

Several winding walks form an alternative way to return to Babbacombe for the energetic, or in the winter months when the cliff railway is closed. There are superb views across Lyme Bay from the clifftops, and Portland Bill can be seen on a clear day.

BABBACOMBE

THE BEACH 1925 / 78445

After the railway reached Newton Abbot in 1846, it soon acquired a reputation as a Victorian railway town. A great deal of building took place during the years that followed; the population increased three-fold during Queen Victoria's reign.

NEWTON ABBOT

THE GLOBE HOTEL AND ST LEONARD'S TOWER

1906 / 56573

TEIGNMOUTH

THE PARADE 1903 / 49559

The sea wall leads to the Parson and Clerk rocks, with the railway—surely one of the loveliest stretches of line in the country—running alongside. On stormy days the sea washes over both this path and the speeding trains.

TEIGNMOUTH

THE TERRACE WALK 1911 / 63698

These whale bones were brought to the town by a local trader, a reminder of Teignmouth's importance as a port. Local sailing ships would sail regularly across the Atlantic, bound for Newfoundland and other American destinations. The whale bones are no longer in position.

TEIGNMOUTH

WHALE BONES 1922 / 73089

A place familiar to all train travellers through Devon, Dawlish nestles across the sides of a broad combe, with the railway line protecting the town from the sea. The resort gets its name from the dark stream, 'doflisc' in Anglo-Saxon, which now runs through the resort's central parkland. Dawlish began as two discreet hamlets, one inland by the parish church and another on the seashore, but quickly grew as the first visitors arrived to holiday in the late 18th century.

DAWLISH

THE SEAFRONT FROM THE ROYAL HOTEL 1890 / 26059

DAWLISH

BOAT COVE 1925 / 78437

The coves around Dawlish and Teignmouth were used extensively by smugglers until Isambard Kingdom Brunel built his atmospheric railway line and the accompanying cliff tunnels in the first half of the 19th century, making the landing of cargoes more difficult.

DAWLISH

THE BEACH 1922 / 72990

After 1803 the environs of the Dawlish Water were landscaped to provide the kind of pleasure grounds expected in fashionable resorts of this period. Today the stream is a haven for wildlife, including Dawlish's famous black swans.

DAWLISH

THE LAWNS 1925 / 78441

The Dawlish Water and its high tributary the Smallacombe Brook rise on the wooded heathland of Little Haldon Hill, which rises 800 feet at the back of the town. Walking the length of the Water was a favourite excursion for early visitors, and can still be enjoyed today.

DAWLISH

DAWLISH WATER 1928 / 81171

The old Turf Lock Inn stands near the lock gates where the Exeter Canal—probably the oldest in England—meets the Exe estuary. This popular public house can be reached only by boat, bicycle or on foot—cars are not allowed on the narrow track across Exminster marshes.

EXMINSTER

TURF LOCK 1906 / 53983

THE EAST DEVON COAST

THE EXE estuary, a paradise for birdwatchers, forms a formidable barrier between Teignbridge and East Devon. And perhaps it is just as well, for both the geography and character of this next stretch of coastline are very different from anything we have seen so far. Even its resort towns—Exmouth, Budleigh Salterton, and Sidmouth—have a sedate, old-fashioned feel that the Torbay resorts have probably lost for ever.

This is not surprising, given that Exmouth is the oldest watering place in Devon. Seaside holidays were almost invented there, and even with its present massive influx of holidaymakers, it has managed to retain the air of dignity it probably enjoyed during the Regency, when Lady Byron and Lady Nelson were typical of the illustrious guests who enjoyed its varied delights.

A little further along the coast, where the tide plays fitfully with its beach of large round stones, or 'pobbles', is Budleigh Salterton, often unfairly labelled as a seaside retirement home for aged colonels; here, you might expect to see Noel Coward or Miss Marple pacing the streets. The label is an unkind and rather hoary local joke, for the folk are friendly and younger than you might imagine, even if the town itself seems to be a habitation by the sea rather than anything like a traditional holiday resort. But with the delightful coastal scenery and the placid waters of the River Otter to explore, who needs artificial entertainments anyway?

Sidmouth occupies a broad green valley where the long line of red sandstone cliffs breaks to admit the departure of the tiny River Sid. Queen Victoria spent some of her childhood here in the company of her impoverished parents, and always held the town in high regard. It is as good a centre as anywhere else to explore the wild and unspoiled hinterland of East Devon, with its coastal footpaths and long stretches of lonely heathland.

Between the resorts are miles of secluded and dramatic coastline, broken occasionally by old smuggling villages such as Branscombe and Beer. Even as late as the 19th century Jack Rattenbury, the 'Rob Roy of the West', ran the landings of night cargo hereabouts, surviving to gain a pension, write a book of memoirs, and pass away more peacefully than some of his fellows. His contemporary Ambrose Stapleton was the parson of East Budleigh, but the ringleader of a smuggling gang for all that. Over at Sidmouth the entire tribe of the Mutter family seemed to have dabbled with the illicit trade. Many a villager in East Devon must have 'watched the wall, my darling' while the gentlemen went by. Contraband was hidden in the tombs of Branscombe churchyard; one unfortunate customs officer lies there as well, having 'slipped' over a cliff. As far as the landscape goes, little has really changed since those hard but romantic days.

LYMPSTONE

1896 / 37645

As the red cliffs turn to white chalk on the journey eastwards, the coastline dips past the towns of Seaton and Axmouth, where the wind blows through the reeds of the silted Axe estuary. Beyond is the great landslip where hundreds of acres of cliff tumbled into the sea early in the 19th century. Here East Devon merges imperceptibly with West Dorset, and our long journey along the county's southern coast comes to an end.

EXMOUTH

ROLLE STREET 1895 / 36055

At the beginning of the last millennium, marauding Danes landed
on these sandy Devon beaches and put the village of Exmouth to
fire and sword. But the settlement rose from the ashes; in the year
1347 it was wealthy enough to contribute ten vessels to attack
Calais. Its maritime activities continue to this day.

EXMOUTH

THE SANDS 1890 / 26261

Exmouth is still a busy little port, though merchant vessels are now outnumbered by sailing boats. A ferry crosses the Exe from here to the village of Starcross on the opposite bank.

EXMOUTH

THE PIER 1896 / 37624

EXMOUTH

VIEW FROM THE BEACON 1925 / 78594

Exmouth's long sea front and sandy beaches made sea-bathing a popular recreation from the town's earliest days as a resort. Tourists came for the bracing air and social activities. Some, such as Lady Nelson, widow of the Admiral, never left. She lies buried in the churchyard at nearby Littleham.

The estuary of the River Exe around Topsham is one of the finest places in Britain for bird-watching. Regular cruises take enthusiasts down-river to see the famous avocets on the river's mud banks. These fisherfolk and boat-men share a rare idle moment in a busy day.

TOPSHAM

THE QUAY 1906 / 53990

Topsham, which is at the head of the Exe estuary, became a seaport of considerable importance in the Middle Ages. Trade with Holland led to the building of many of the Dutch-style gabled houses that line the Strand.

TOPSHAM

THE STRAND 1906 / 53993

Budleigh Salterton stands to the west of the silted estuary of the River Otter. Its own beach is sandless and full of large pebbles, which seem to sing as the tides play across them. It gets its name from the salterns, or salt pans, used by the monks of nearby Otterton Priory.

BUDLEIGH SALTERTON

THE PROMENADE 1898 / 42448

Sidmouth's sea wall was first built in the 1830s, though the attempts to create a satisfactory harbour failed. Fashionable hotels soon lined the front, with villa residences and smart cottages being erected along the slopes of Sid Vale to cater for a dramatic increase in the resident population.

SIDMOUTH

THE ESPLANADE 1918 / 68739

In the early years of the 19th century the impoverished Duke of
Kent came to live at Woolbrook Glen. He died at the house in
1820, though not before he had taken his baby daughter in his arms
to see the sea, boasting to locals 'one day she will be your queen'.
Many years later, Queen Victoria placed a window in the parish
church as a monument to the father who had loved her so much.

SIDMOUTH

LOOKING WEST 1924 / 76360

SIDMOUTH

FORE STREET 1904 / 52071

Sidmouth began as a small fishing town with a bustling local market, but even these activities had begun to decline by the time the first visitors arrived in the late 18th century. As with many similar resorts, the Napoleonic Wars boosted Sidmouth's fortunes, with so many people being forced to holiday at home. Here we see a coach-and-four taking visitors on an excursion.

In the 1930s Sidmouth acquired a reputation as an upmarket holiday resort, not so much for its sea-bathing or its beach as for the tranquillity of its setting and the mildness of its climate. In the distance we see the great cliff of High Peak—one of the highest points along the Devon coast.

SIDMOUTH

THE ESPLANADE AND THE BEACH 1934 / 86238

Beer was the birthplace in 1788 of the smuggler Jack Rattenbury, who lived a life of adventure landing untaxed cargoes along much of the Devon coast. The old rogue lived to a respectable, though gout-ridden, old age, writing his memoirs and receiving a small pension from the respectable local worthy Lord Rolle, who admired the wily Jack's nerve—and may have received a keg of brandy in return.

BEER

THE VILLAGE 1892 / 31318

BEER

PILLOW LACE WORKERS 1901 / 47861

This picturesque village and cove has always attracted the eye of artist and photographer. One Victorian guide book writer described Beer as 'a rare subject for the pencil'. The notable Victorian artist Hamilton Macallum settled in Beer, and exhibited many local scenes at the Royal Academy in London. It was also a noted centre for lace-making.

BEER

FISHING BOATS 1918 / 68702

Seaton is a mostly Victorian town hard by the mouth of the River Axe. Though never one of Devon's more fashionable resorts, it has a charm of its own and an attractive setting. The strange colours, white and red, of the cliffs around the town give a striking effect when the sun falls upon them. They are notoriously crumbly, and rock falls are common.

SEATON

WHITE CLIFF FROM THE BEACH 1898 / 42425

The end of our coastal journey brings us to one of the finest churches in Devon. Axmouth's St Michael's is a delight. Originally early Norman in style, it was altered and enlarged in 1330, and a perpendicular tower was added in the 15th century. Axmouth, the last coastal community wholly in Devon, was an important port until its river entrance silted up.

AXMOUTH

THE VILLAGE 1927 / 79802

INDEX

PLEASE HELP US BRING FRITH'S
PHOTOGRAPHS TO LIFE

Our authors do their best to recount the history of the places they write about. They give insights into how particular towns and villages developed, they describe the architecture of streets and buildings, and they discuss the lives of famous people who lived there. But however knowledgeable our authors are, the story they tell is necessarily incomplete.

Frith's photographs are so much more than plain historical documents. They are living proofs of the flow of human life down the generations. They show real people at real moments in history; and each of those people is the son or daughter of someone, the brother or sister, aunt or uncle, grandfather or grandmother of someone else. All of them lived, worked and played in the streets depicted in Frith's photographs.

We would be grateful if you would tell us about the many places shown in our photographs—the streets with their buildings, shops, businesses and industries. Describe your own memories of life in those streets: what it was like growing up there, who ran the local shop and what shopping was like years ago; if your workplace is shown tell us about your working day and what the building is used for now. With your help more and more Frith photographs can be brought to life, and vital memories preserved for posterity.

We will gradually add your comments and stories to the archive for the benefit of historians of the future. Wherever possible, we will try to include some of your comments in future editions of our books. Moreover, if you spot errors in dates, titles or other facts, please let us know, because our archive records are not always completely accurate—they rely on 150 years of human endeavour and hand-compiled records.

So please write, fax or email us with your stories and memories. Thank you!

CHOOSE ANY PHOTOGRAPH FROM THIS BOOK

for your FREE Mounted Print. Order further prints at half price

Fill in and cut out the voucher on the next page and return it with your remittance for £2.50 for postage, packing and handling to UK addresses (US $5.00 for USA and Canada). For all other overseas addresses include £5.00 post and handling. Choose any photograph included in this book. Make sure you quote its unique reference number eg. 42365 (it is mentioned after the photograph date. 1890 / 42365). Your SEPIA print will be approx 12" x 8" and mounted in a cream mount with a burgundy rule line (overall size 14" x 11").

Mounted Print
Overall size 14 x 11 inches

Order additional Mounted Prints at HALF PRICE - If you would like to order more Frith prints from this book, possibly as gifts for friends and family, you can buy them at half price (with no extra postage and handling costs) - only £7.49 each (UK orders), US $14.99 each (USA and Canada).

---

* IMPORTANT!

These special prices are only available if you order at the same time as you order your free mounted print. You must use the ORIGINAL VOUCHER on the facing page (no copies permitted). We can only despatch to one address.

Have your Mounted Prints framed (UK orders only) - For an extra £14.95 per print you can have your mounted print(s) framed in an elegant polished wood and gilt moulding, overall size 16" x 13" (no additional postage).

FRITH PRODUCTS AND SERVICES

All Frith photographs are available for you to buy as framed or mounted prints. From time to time, other illustrated items such as Address Books, Calendars, Table Mats are also available. Already, almost 50,000 Frith archive photographs can be viewed and purchased on the internet through the Frith website.

For more detailed information on Frith companies and products, visit

www.francisfrith.co.uk

For further information, trade, or author enquiries, contact:

The Francis Frith Collection, Frith's Barn, Teffont, Salisbury SP3 5QP

Tel: +44 (0) 1722 716 376 Fax: +44 (0) 1722 716 881 Email: sales@francisfrith.co.uk

Voucher

*for FREE
and Reduced Price
Frith Prints*

*Do not photocopy this voucher. Only the original is valid, so please fill it in,
cut it out and return it to us with your order.*

	Picture ref no	Page number	Qty	Mounted @ £7.49 UK @$14.99 US	Framed + £14.95 (UK only)	US orders Total $	UK orders Total £
1			1	Free of charge*	£	$	£
2				£7.49 ($14.99)	£	$	£
3				£7.49 ($14.99)	£	$	£
4				£7.49 ($14.99)	£	$	£
5				£7.49 ($14.99)	£	$	£
				£7.49 ($14.99)	£	$	£
Please allow 28 days for delivery				* Post & handling		$5.00	£2.50
				Total Order Cost		US $	£

Title of this book . . . .

I enclose a cheque / postal order (UK) for £ . . . . $ . . . .
payable to 'Francis Frith Collection' (USA orders 'Frith USA Inc')

OR debit my Mastercard / Visa / Switch (UK) / Amex card / Discover (USA)
(credit cards only on non UK and US orders), card details below

Card Number

Issue No (Switch only)   Valid from (Amex/Switch)

Expires   Signature

Name Mr/Mrs/Ms . . . .

Address . . . .

. . . .

. . . .

Postcode/Zip. . . . . Country . . . .

Daytime Tel No . . . .   Valid to 31/12/06

PAYMENT CURRENCY: We only accept payment in £ Sterling or US $.
If you are ordering **from any other country, please pay by credit
card**, and you will be charged in one of these currencies.